THEM!

Gary Fincke

Červená Barva Press
Somerville, Massachusetts

Červená Barva Press

P.O. Box 440357

W. Somerville, MA 02144

www.cervenabarvapress.com

Bookstore: www.thelostbookshelf.com

Cover Art: Shannon Fincke

Cover Design: William J. Kelle

Author Photo: Jonathan MacBride

Production: Allison O'Keefe

ISBN: 978-1-950063-52-9

ACKNOWLEDGMENTS

Many of these poems, often in much different form, appeared in the following journals: *Poetry Northwest, The Literary Review, North American Review, The Laurel Review, Zone 3, American Journal of Poetry, The Widener Review, Mankato Poetry Review, Proem, The Blue Guitar,* and *The Cresset.*

"The Night of the Lepus" and "They Saved Hitler's Brain" appeared in the anthology *MovieWorks* (Little Theater Press, 1990)

"Zombies" and "In Films, the Army Ants are Always Intelligent" appeared in the collection *Standing around the Heart* (University of Arkansas, 2005)

"The Deadly Mantis" (as "Perspective") appeared in the collection *The Mussolini Diaries* (Serving House, 2020)

CONTENTS

THEM!

I Married a Monster from Outer Space

He has to marry her. Nothing
Unusual in that, loveless
For the sake of children,
But think of going home
To the horror of something
That can't leave you alone.

How did he get into this skin?
No star-flight boot camp
For invasion had prepared him
For this bad luck, drawing
The short straw of beauty
As his extraterrestrial duty.

Lust, arousal, foreplay—
His mind's being fed by a fool.
Everything in his head is
Thighs and lips, breasts and hips,
But something's not getting through;
She's pliable as fish, smooth

As a nausea of eggs, and
Finally, he's sick of acting.
Outside of town, in the spaceship,
Is the man who wants to drown
Under her, smother her from above—
Telepathy can be reversed.

Let him listen for a while
As he walks upstairs to bed,
His body changing to knobs
And ridges, his face to tubes.
He knows that every planet
Has fables of tested love,

And just then, before he turns
The corner, he hears her
Undressing, and he breathes
One moment from the reason
For exploring, spending all
Of those light years on travel.

In Films, the Army Ants are Always Intelligent

Water and fire again, we think, watching
Natives dig a trench, lug the gasoline
To its banks. It's the white man's solution,
Some land owner protecting investments,
All those years of cheap labor just lately
Paying off. Ants, after all, are ants, but
Understandably, he's a bit nervous
When his workers chant, fumble with magic
In a pouch. Savages, he's learned, always
Sense when the absentee gods should be called.

And we might wonder, while the cameras pan
The rain forest for troops, if these things rest,
If there's a day along the Amazon
When you could sleep off hard work or a drunk
In safety. And why there's still a jungle;
And why these ants, a million years of them,
Haven't eaten every square inch of green.
There's never a natural predator;
There's only the good sense of travel north
So climate can negotiate with them.

All we're taught, at last, are the miles of them,
That their sign language ripples front to back,
Reaching the billionth soldier correctly.
Remember that schoolroom game, the one where
Miss Harshman whispered a message into
Janey's ear? She turned and whispered those words
To Billy who whispered to Sally and
Thirty seats later you recited them
To laughter that blossomed from the first row?

Think of yourself as sluggard in the rear.
For days, you've had nothing to eat, the ground
You're covering stripped clean ten thousand ranks
Before you. Well, somebody has to starve,
You might conclude, improvisational
In the tropics. But then you feel the word,
Sense *plantation, panic, picnic for all.*
So, there's sacrifice ahead; there's something
To those parables, you see, when your turn
Finally comes: The early waves were burnt;
The first leaf rafts were sunk; and you're certain,
Dancing before battle, that the water
And fire are gone, that the natives have fled
Or been shot in the back by the owner.
So he's on his own now, self-destructive,
Or maybe he has dynamite, something
Apocalyptic. On the other side
Of the moat, there is feasting. All you have
To do is cross, stepping from one body
To another, to cultivated land.

Invasion of the Body Snatchers

After the world slid into soulless,
After the pods had replicated
Even the stars of the movie,
After we left the theater and drove
To the music of favorite scenes,
My eight-year old son tumbled
Into bed after sparring with
His Darth Vader punching bag—
A tall, costumed, weighted balloon
That could take a punch, returning
To upright like a contender.

Or an alien pod, one that woke
Him to crying, "Am I changed?"
Nothing consoled him, not lights
Turned on, not an examination
Of Vader's familiar plastic face,
How a pod-father would pretend
The world hadn't changed after
His real body had been absorbed
By monsters, leaving him an orphan,
Even when Vader was deflated,
Even when I let him search
The garbage for my former self.

The Attack of the Fifty-Foot Woman

Their first question is about sex.
The aliens, puzzled, want to watch,
But they've only beamed up Allison,
And they're way too large to suit her.
Sure, she says, a man would help, but
"My husband's out screwing some bitch.
Release me, and I'll show you something
About how justice works on Earth."

She gets her way. She feels enormous
Thinking of what her man has coming,
How those monsters will understand.
It's nothing at all to switch sizes—
She's known the ten feet of happiness,
The limitless reach of jealousy.

Although now Allison has to wear
The same old ratty dress, the one made
From miracle fibers that don't fray
At the seams. "Where's Harry?" she screams.
"Where's that doll-sized man of mine?" She'll shake
Some sense into him; she'll show him
What the King Kong myth is all about.

But there's a problem and she knows it:
Talk about irreconcilable differences—
So what if this midget were squashed?
So what if she found a dwarf who'd be true?
You'd get angry, too, guess those giants
Wanted you for more than research.

And now there's no privacy. She's followed
Everywhere she goes. She thinks urine.
And worse. Christ, there's always a catch
To growth. Where are those power lines?
The snapping toy planes? Something must
Show up soon to halt her alien rage.

Them! . . . and . . . Tarantula!

"Close your eyes!" Aunt Margaret said.
Across from the Homestead Theater
The sidewalk swarmed with strikers
Buzzing *hell* and *damn*. "Like this," she said,
Slapping her hands to her ears,
But I heard *bitch* and *bastard* before
She bought our way inside where
Huge ants were screaming at flame throwers,
Working their claws as they burned.
"The End" said we'd entered an hour late.
In minutes, a huge spider
Stalked the screaming until it, too, was
Fire-bombed, this time from a jet.
The previews promised two comedies,
Double westerns, paired romance.
When the ants returned, my aunt muttered,
"We know what happens to Them,"
Tugged me to the door beside the screen.
Over my head, a woman
Ten times my size stood hypnotized by
A set of enormous eyes.
Outside, at twilight, the strike-closed mill
Had turned radioactive,
Emptied by the bomb. Lifting their signs,
The men spread into traffic.
"Them!" my aunt said, as if steelworkers
Were giants, as if they would
Destroy Pittsburgh and devour us all.

The Curse of the Demon

My mother sets her alarm for five a.m.
My father slides the first bread from his ovens.
Exactly midnight, Friday, the first "Who's there?"
Of the stalked, this demon, so far, all smoke
And footprints, its curse passed like the dollars
My mother presses into late chapters
Of books she gives me. Soon, the crescendo
Of a conjured storm wakes her. "Sandwich buns,"
She says. "He's nearly to Parker House rolls."
Smoke flies and folds in on itself; the caped host
Cackles her back to bed. At the moment for
The power of runic symbols, my father,
I know, is on sweet rolls and coffee cakes,
Working through the specific schedule she loves.
The magician sprawls beside a speeding train,
His demon materializing as huge
As collective memory, and I know, watching,
This monster was added after the film's release,
Someone believing we needed to witness.

1965, Watching Poe at the Belmar

We weren't far from home. A few miles.
A bridge. Homewood, like any part
Of Pittsburgh Jack and I imagined, was
Close enough for his father's Peugeot.
We knew enough French to understand
Both halves of the owner's manual and
Parked so close to the marquee I said,
"Dans rue grise des ruines," expecting
Broken, empty seats, a janitor hobbling
The aisle with an early broom and bag
While Vincent Price let loose his laugh
During both movies we were seeing for
Under a dollar in nineteen sixty-five.

The truth? That theater was packed
When we entered in the dark, minutes
Before the House of Usher tumbled.
We whispered in English and slipped
Into the first vacant seats to the right.
We loved every cheesy minute of Poe,
Especially Monsieur Valdemar melting
Into phantasmagoric gore, but when
The lights went up, we saw ourselves
As white as our hazy idea of Grace.
The aisle clotted, black and loud,
All the dead or rescued white
Actors already hammered dark
By the projectionist's thumb.

In that aisle, we didn't have names,
But we worked the crowd's rhythm
So perfectly into our shoes we bumped
Nobody in that swirl, impeding none
Of the three hundred black patrons
Who never saw us, we believed,

Walking speechless into the cataract
Gray of midnight, snow surviving
Among the tracks all of us made
Toward three cars and the doors
Of a hundred houses spreading
Into the January darkness.

The next summer, despite love
And family, rows of those homes
Would fall to the fire of riots,
And someone in that Belmar crowd
Would kill or be killed for honor,
Pride, or insanity, though Jack and I
Wouldn't know anything but
The filmed version, the two
Of us, at the end of the era
Of the double feature, experts
On Poe who compared, scornful,
Once we had driven four blocks
From the Belmar's shabby screen,
What we'd read to what we'd seen.

They Saved Hitler's Brain

Since Berlin fell, Hitler's bobbed south
Of here, counting, for his comeback,
On surgeons. He's sick of floating
In a jar, practicing Spanish.
And what's worse, these brown shirts believe
He's kept his voice, a miracle,
That, behind glass, he's bilingual,
Not a ventriloquist's Fuhrer
Tied to tape-recorded flashbacks.

It's like religion, this long shot
In the tropics, splicing the hell
In us to a new set of nerves –
Though there's plenty of fascist flags
And open borders, quick response
To the casting call for bodies
To house this shabby, beeswax brain.

All of these bowl-cuts and salutes;
Mustaches, goose-steps, and sieg-heils –
They listen, practice, dream and wait
By his aquarium until
One of them is chosen. And when
Eyelids flutter and fingers twitch,
All around the room, from white gown
To white gown, the identical
Dream skitters and stops, clutches, holds.

Zombies

It was the year of zombie movies, dead bodies
Without brains that wanted the blood of the living—

It was the year, at my school, of five student deaths,
The principal acknowledging three of them through
Counseling, assemblies, and a week of silent
Moments for the Regents scholar, the soccer star,
And the girl who checked my groceries after school.

One of the two whose deaths were not announced was killed
On a motorcycle, thrown into a phone pole
After a skid and rollover. The other, drunk,
Stumbled in front of a truck, their names short-listed
With the absentees under *Deceased: Please Delete.*
They didn't read, those boys whose deaths were not announced.
They didn't listen, those boys, "And truthfully now,"
The principal said, "are you going to miss them?"

It was the year of the dead who wanted to eat
The brains of the living, the natural logic
Of the empty head. How easily hatreds talked
And talked. There were teachers who read that absence list
Like a stock report, cheering extended illness.
The friends of those boys said nothing about silence
In homeroom, a day off, or an oak tree planted
In memory. They kept hate to themselves until
They could drink it into speech among themselves—slurs
Spoken in cars, expletives underage in bars,
The curses that followed fists to the stunned faces
Of each other, not to the principal's they loathed,
The teachers' they'd delete, if there was any choice
In who lived and died in the lottery of luck.

That boy whose brains were spilled against a roadside post,
That boy whose brains were splattered under a truck tire—
All along they'd been brainless in the back of class,
But I thought of them rising when Three Mile Island
Leaked into our lives; I thought of the school downwind,
The dead getting second chance by radiation
The way they do in B-movies, the principal
Keeping the school in session the full day because
He believed (Who wouldn't? he said) the spokesperson.
When, the next week, I dialed in sick from Virginia,
I knew he'd call my house, checking, on the third day.
Which didn't matter, since those boys, looking for brains,
Would crack his skull and slurp him down. Wasn't he smart?
Hadn't he known all along how they would turn out?

Night of the Lepus

"I don't want to alarm you folks, but there's a herd
of killer rabbits on the way."

Maybe Jimmy Carter would have panicked
When the sheriff announced his news,
But not one of the extras does. There's no
Adrenalin rushed by the rabbit threat;
There's nothing but the fire drill
Forward surge of schoolchildren who
Obey to be paid and have their faces on
The screen at a weed-choked drive-in.
You'd think someone should have known
Not to premise the bunnies carnivorous
And huge. Just let them mate. Protect
Each one from predators. Those sweet
Litters of multiplication will wish
Your hands on their fur, your fingers
Under their chins, and while you sleep
They'll smother you. And talk about
Typecast: Here's Janet Leigh mouthing
Her stabbed-in-the-shower scream, but
These rabbits don't remember Mother.
In the Bates Motel of the prairie,
These killers should hop from room to room
And, slow-motioned, pillow their destruction.

Damnation Alley

The Parasitoid wasp can survive more than four times the radiation that a roach can.

After the war, "flesh stripping cockroaches"
reigned in Salt Lake City, not only
surviving like science says, but mutated
huge and deadly. Decades by now, that myth
of roaches as what will outlive us,
the prophecy resting in the bellies
of airplanes and silos, inside the holds
of submarines ceaselessly circling while
we've memorized our extinction details
of lives banished from the lost planet
of loathsome insects who love the dark.

How we've shuddered reading Revelation
in the Postmodern Testament, but now
we learn that promise won't be kept,
that when everything is poisoned, roaches
dead as well, just these wasps will go on,
the world humming with last thing, some
Jeremiah of atomic war foretelling the world
Without us, a hell of crawling replaced
by a hell of flight swarming the ruins.

One afternoon, my daughter, eight years old,
memorized the definition of *swarm*
as she flailed at a thick flurry of wasps.
In one day, I've spoken *swarm* when I saw
ants at our sidewalk cracks, the fruit flies
surrounding our garbage, caterpillars
incubating inside translucent tents
on our blossoming decorative trees,
any of those gatherings sufficient
to terrorize us with numbers, the way,

in crowded foreign cities, the jabber
of a language we do not understand
becomes a buzz or a drone or even,
the definitive sound of the future.

The Man with the X-Ray Eyes

"I'm closing in on the gods,"
the doctor says, his motives
nothing less than noble—
saving lives by advancing
science--but his hubris
the equal of any hero
in the Shakespeare canon.

Naturally, we root hard
as he risks his own eyes
with experimental drops,
but no sooner do we cheer
his success than we sense
that the arc of this quest
will lurch toward catharsis.

Super-powered, he discovers
the pleasure of the x-ray vision
promised by comic book ads.
Gambling is a cinch, every
card exposed. While women
provocatively do The Twist,
he strips them with his eyes.

Like the Classics remind us,
there's no limit to what pride
demands, preparing to ruin
the best of us. What follows
is the comeuppance that Act V
yields for a hero obsessed with
seeing "farther than time itself."

Now, earthly visions exhausted,
there is only somewhere beyond
the sky to find where God's eye

is watching, no salvation left
but the Oedipus solution,
the doctor doing penance by
reaching for his offending eyes.

The Biblical Epic, with Intermission

Some Sunday evenings, while I sat
Between my parents like a prisoner,
God was the deep voice that shook trees
And billowed the cloaks of bearded men.
Jesus was the back of a head
Or a lifted hand, their stories so long,
We watched them, during the double
Feature era, one by one, talking
Through intermission, shutting up for
The last halves of the holy films.
Suffer the little children, Christ said,
But soon he was suffering, too.
My mother passed me ham sandwiches,
Poured me milk from her blue thermos.
When Jesus turned, his white robe fluttered
At his top-of-the-screen cut throat,
His voice issuing soft sermons from the void.
The New Testament women were
Never blonde; only the heathen showed
Their breasts to Christ. I didn't know
If he looked when the lost leaned forward,
If his eyes shifted down despite
The tilt of his holy, upturned head.

The Mesa of Lost Women

The mesa, we're told, is in Mexico,
the last convincing detail within
the next eighty minutes of science
familiarly mad. By now, we know
the doctor is played by Jackie Coogan,
four decades removed from being
The Kid, his parents pissing away
so much of the fortune he made
as a child that a new law, too late
for him, deters such moms and dads.
Look, who wouldn't, after a life
of litigation, love to play crazy,
showing off your new-found skills?
Who wouldn't want to create
an army of powerful women,
especially ones who will have
no remorse? Doing the slow,
hypnotic Dance of Destruction,
one tight-dressed, spider-infused
subject invites us into a weird,
unknown world filled with strange
exotic women born without souls.
Last week, we saw the previews,
their promises irresistible. We expect
the lost women to swarm and destroy
in a war against unbelieving man.

The Day of the Triffids

The year he turned twelve, summer stuffed with science fiction movies and books, the unpaved road below the boy's house split along the shoulder, guardrails slumping level with the gravel. Nearby, a dump deepened with tires and trash, appliances, mattresses. Beyond it, the state game land was a place, when entered, to gather fear like berries. When leaves smothered the sky, he was underwater; when branches snapped, the played-out mines were graves, his mother's "Never alone in there" insistent as a smoke alarm.

In July, he was in love with the Triffids, the alien trees that advanced like guerillas after the world went blind from watching a meteor shower. The forest became malignant. The Triffids flourished in the Earth's soil and had an appetite for all those sightless humans. He watched it twice.

The paths he followed in the game lands were half-eaten by locust and sumac. Just outside of its boundaries, mine entrances were labeled like poisons; a thin canal carried runoff to dunes of silt.

On screen, the Triffids were so easily killed by salt water, they might have arrived from West Oz. The world was saved. Every tree in the woods was rooted or dead. When August began, the boy read the novel, where nothing in the final scenes ended those aliens, even on the last page.

One late afternoon, among a thick stand of pine trees, the boy found a striped shirt and black socks soaked and faintly rotten as if they had wintered there. The shirt hung so small in his hands, that whoever had worn it began to scream. The boy listened hard for heavy steps. He checked the trees for movement.

And yes, although nothing happened except fantasy following him home, he picked up a heavy branch and carried it toward the road, clutching it like bravery. In his room, the novel still lying beside his bed, the boy closed his eyes and sat in his wooden chair that strangers had cut and shaped and fitted into something so common that one would always surround him. He kept his eyes shut until he cried.

Beach Girls and the Monster aka Monster from the Surf

Just before we get impatient with
the first scene's surfside dancing,
one of the bikini girls wanders away
alone, and everyone at the drive-in
knows she's victim number one
for the monster that is covered
with so much kelp we think of
streamers dangling from the gym
rafters at the homecoming dance.

It's not gory or even very scary,
but shortly after the killing,
an oceanographer bends over
to examine marks in the sand.
"It looks like the print of the deadly
Fantigua fish," he pronounces,
verisimilitude disappearing. "It's not
the claw print of any fish in this area."

Grown old, it's Ramar of the Jungle,
one of my grade school TV heroes,
playing the professor, who, unmasked,
is found inside that surf-monster outfit.
He's chosen mass murder to discourage
beach parties so his son will give up
drinking, girls, and rock and roll,
a lost cause, for sure. At last,
without mask, yet still costumed,
he loses control of his speeding MG,
plunging over a cliff because
he's trying to steer with the claws
of the deadly Fantigua fish.

That's it. Though even a glance
reveals that the plummeting car
looks nothing like the MG, just
some boxy junk-heap. But wait--even
the car that explodes is yet
another lifted from stock footage,
the MG, most likely, already
safely returned to its owner.

The End, right? But not quite.
That bikini girl, nine year later,
is resurrected. She shimmies
to an instrumental version
of the same miserable song
and, learning nothing, wanders off
again, the monster from the surf
lurking nearby, the entire movie,
retitled and repackaged to unspool
for the eyes of the unsuspecting.

War of the Worlds: the Broadcasts

One evening, my father repeated the story
Of the night fire invaded his bakery where
Wires shorted near the blue refrigerator.
One evening, we stood on the sidewalk
While he named the seventeen weeds
In the vacant lot of progress, that building sold
And burned by the controlled fire of investors.
I watched that empty space as if it were shielded
By the force-field of aliens like the Martians
Orson Welles had conjured the year my father
Was hired by a baker whose breath was shortened
By the invasion of emphysema.
One evening, we parked across the alley
While my father said he was lucky his lungs
Had stayed clear despite the clouds of flour,
That his one deaf ear had kept him from the war
In 1944, the same year, I'd learned,
The War of the Worlds had been rebroadcast
In Santiago, Chile, six years
And publicity doing nothing to stop
The heart attacks and injuries of panic.
One evening, that lot paved and lined for parking,
My father said it took that owner a decade
To die, that the baker's widow had signed
The sales receipt, and I didn't say a word
About how, in 1949, in Quito,
Someone else reread that radio play,
And the spooked, sick of being duped, set fire
To the station, killing twenty people,
The earthlings watching the panicked tumble
From upstairs windows, what invaders deserved.
Each of those evenings, my father detailed
1950, the year his fire was broadcast
By the community bell coded to name
Which street and block, the year he guided me,

Age five, through what was salvaged, teaching me
What can be lost and the necessity
Of rebuilding despite the threats that attack
From clouds because, "before you know it,
The Communists will come," as if he meant
Me to realize they wanted to burn us out,
That if the air exploded, saving ourselves
Depended upon these small rehearsals
For the inevitability of an angry God.

Emanuelle and the Last Cannibals

Soft-core with cannibals,
A natural, the film crew
Creating a jungle where
Everything suggests sex
And slaughter, but it's hard
Doing this sort of gore and sex,
The actors understandably
Nervous, all the tasty parts
Of themselves exposed.
The women rightly cringe
When their breasts are fondled
Like possible portions.
They think weight and heft,
Forget about feigned lust
And heavy breathing when
Proffered lips turn threatening.
And worse, the men shrink
And retreat from the women's
Practiced tongues until
The close-ups show nothing
But the sad, flaccid facts
Of a nudist nursing home.
So, the cannibals get more
Screen time. They take their teeth
And knives to the sheep's heart,
The pig's liver, and the long
Rope of goat's entrails,
Sucking and slurping, smiling
And satisfied, doing take
After take until every bit
Of that glistening flesh is gone.

Rock, Rock, Rock! . . . *and* . . . The Girl Can't Help It

Thirteen, along the central street
Through Etna, I joined, near
Midnight, a few dozen patrons
Of the Friday double feature
Split into the singles and groups
Of going home. Frankie Lymon,
Thirteen, had sung a doo-wop tune
While my mother drove my father
To his work with pastry and bread.
Tuesday Weld, thirteen, had looked sick
About the neckline of her dark,
Strapless dress while Jayne Mansfield's
Magnificent breasts had spilled out
And filled the theater's wide screen.
My mother was slicing apples
For coffee cakes while I counted
The thirteen hundred steps to her
Along Main Street where a man asked,
Getting in stride, what I felt when
I watched that cleavage stop just short
Of the nipples. Ahead of us,
A couple entered the one car
In the bank's lot. Its headlights swept
The father and son of us, smeared
The soot-caked mill, and faced away,
Like I did, saying the quick words
Of "nothing much." I'd never heard
The serious sentence after
"I thought so," but he repeated
The brief phrase like a chorus.
My parents were talking six blocks
From his hands. The car lot was full
Of dark alleys among its Fords,
And I thought, "Keep walking, Gary,
Keep walking," while music squawked

From a watchman's approaching radio
Until his flashlight quickened my feet
Toward that night's sliced apples, ones
My mother had quartered for me,
Peeled and sweet, running her knife through
The sink's warm water before she
Wiped it clean and drove us toward home.

Incubus

Swollen on camera,
a woman claims Satan,
disguised as her husband,
drove home after work
and abused her. How clever,
she says, my helpmate
a pastor, these bruises
twice awful from devil's fists.

Within a week, walking
nearsighted by the school
they attend, I've mistaken
my son and my daughter
for strangers, both calling
to me from a limbo of fog.

And only this morning,
I measured the pre-dawn
like an Easter priest,
something walking the yard,
something taking a minute
with the door, yet the dog
refusing to bark.

Whatever was below me
needed no lights, declined
the stairs. The dog, so like
the one who's lived here ten years,
circled to curl on the carpet.

I waited for footsteps,
the hush of the door to the room
where they'd stay, someone I know
transforming if everything's
possessed in a uniform way.

Wrong Turn

One Friday evening, I sat in a theater,
everyone else under thirty, to watch
a movie on its opening night because
my son's band had a soundtrack song.
Nothing bur horror in West Virginia,
the contemporaries of the audience
dying one by one, each slaughtered
by the unseen who might as well
have been enormous land-sharks
until there were just two survivors,
the couple everyone knew all along
were the only ones with a chance.

We saw the murderous, mutant hillbillies
clearly now. We could gauge the artistry
of the makeup man, and yet, more than
an hour already passed, not one note
of my son's guitar had been heard,
The audience shouted at the screen,
the loudest encouraging the monsters
to rape that last living girl who was,
by now, tied to a bed in the cabin
where the evidence of mass murder
and cannibalism were revealed
by a slow-panning, curious camera.

At last, after the couple escaped,
the inbred mountaineers dead and
thoroughly burned for good measure,
I nearly groaned when the rock song
remained unheard, the credits rolling,
the under-thirty crowd chattering toward
the exits, missing what proved to be
a false ending: an extra arrived
at the wreckage to investigate,

one mutant inexplicably reviving
the way most of this genre's killers do,
the mayhem resuming, sequel likely,
as the opening scream of that song
I've played a hundred times ripped
through the theater, my son's guitar
distorting over additional credits, house
lights gone up to reveal I'm the only one
sitting in his chair as if I'd died of fright.

The Barn of the Naked Dead aka Terror Circus aka Nightmare Circus

No title, it seems, is powerful enough,
but regardless of the opening credit,
three showgirls are always stranded
near Las Vegas, grateful for the help
of a stranger, even if, we soon learn,
he lives, literally, on a nuclear test site.

Well, anyone can guess what isolation
and radiation add up to for this horror.
The barn is full of chained women;
a shed that houses grunts is locked.
By the time the stranger re-enters
as ringmaster with a whip, we know
what sort of acts this circus offers.

And talk about your Pandora's Box,
a wide spectrum of screams escapes
from the mouths of every actress.
Pursuits are plentiful. The ringmaster
needs new acts; a caged panther
gets away; the thing in the flimsy shed,
when it breaks free, is the ringmaster's
hairy, mutated, murderous father let
loose to do terror or nightmare prowling.

Help, we're shown, is on the way, but
the cavalry, this time, arrives a little late
for anything redeeming. By now, most
of the women, as one title claims,
are dead, though none of them have
ever been naked, just partially clothed
like victims in police reports, that phrase,
for promotion, too procedural to drag
anyone into the inexpensive dark
of a second or even third-run theater.

The Deadly Mantis

Yesterday, as if it had knocked,
one mantis on the screen door
at eye-level demanded
a few minutes of shielded,
private welcome for the pastime
of imagining invasion
scaled to ordinary size.

The praying mantis has five eyes: three simple ones lined along the middle of its forehead that probably see only light and dark, and two compound eyes for seeing colors and images.

Time, too, for remembering
the alternate perspective
of B-movies, extravagances
of size featured, once, in each
double feature where radiation
birthed enormous spiders
and ants, lizards, an octopus . . .

Despite its five eyes, the praying mantis is thought to have only one ear, located in a slit in the thorax, which allows the insect to hear ultrasonic sounds.

. . . though in *The Deadly Mantis*,
one Saturday, radiation
was never mentioned while
stock footage showed an iceberg
calving from a glacier
just before the giant mantis,
naturally grown, was freed.

The praying mantis can rotate its triangular heads in almost a full circle, a feature not shared by other insects.

When I watched that film, years later,
with my cousin, he laughed and talked
over the dialogue, his hands often
clutching the air in front of his face.
A child, he said, could create better effects
for "the most dangerous monster that
ever lived!" as it ravaged and devoured.

*When the mantis draws its legs up and folds them under its head, it
resembles a human's praying posture. In actuality, this is the mantis'
hunting position.*

Decades have passed. Whatever
magnifies my cousin's lifelong tics
has settled and gripped. Parkinson's,
perhaps, or some internal wiring
short-circuited to a set of symptoms
pronounced enough to avert my eyes
from his murder of tremors.

*When the mantis sights its prey, it lashes out with its front legs to capture,
then uses the long spikes that line its upper legs to secure, allowing the
mantis to eat at its leisure.*

This morning, I watched the same
or another mantis grasp a hummingbird
at the backyard feeder. In actual size,
the mantis began to chew the bird's head,
appetite guiding it to the brain.
Horrible, and yet I stayed to stare
long past when routine needed me
for inside chores, recollecting
that old B-movie and the spasms,
last week, that prevented my cousin
from passing bread and tossed salad,

the conversation about climate change
that quickly began, hurricanes
and wildfires obscuring the terror
that accompanied the knife and fork.

ABOUT THE AUTHOR

Gary Fincke's books have won The Flannery O'Connor Prize for Short Fiction, the Robert C. Jones Prize for Nonfiction Prose, and what is now the Wheeler Prize for Poetry. His latest collections are *Nothing Falls from Nowhere: Stories* (Steven F. Austin, 2021) and *The Mussolini Diaries* (Serving House, 2020). His new collection of essays *The Mayan Syndrome* will be published later this year by Madhat Press. Its lead essay, "After the Three-Moon Era," was selected to be reprinted in *Best American Essays 2020*.

ABOUT THE ARTIST

Cover artist Shannon Rae Fincke is also an Art Educator and Art Administrator living and working in Los Angeles, CA. Her work has been exhibited at museums and galleries internationally, and has been featured in print, film, and television. She is the Founder/Director of Institute for Visual Arts, mother of three children, and daughter of Gary Fincke.